From **P**astor to **P**astor

Letters of Encouragement and Wisdom

Bob Broadbooks

Love,

Fletch & Julene

Beacon Hill Press of Kansas City
Kansas City, Missouri

Library of Congress Cataloging-in-Publication Data

Broadbooks, Bob, 1951-
    From pastor to pastor : letters of encouragement and wisdom / Bob
Broadbooks.
        p. cm.
    ISBN 0-8341-2041-0 (pbk.)
    1. Pastoral theology. 2. Broadbooks, Bob, 1951—Correspondence. 3.
Wyatt, Doug—Correspondence. 4. Church of the Nazarene—Clergy—
Correspondence. I. Title.

    BV4011.3.B76 2003
    253—dc21

                                                                    2003011065

10 9 8 7 6 5 4 3 2 1

To Pastors

They courageously answer "yes"
to the call of God
and thereby discover
the indescribable joy
of fulfilling the will of God.

Contents

Foreword

I am convinced that a person can't write a credible book on how to play baseball unless he has been a baseball player. An individual can't write a book on "parenting teens through turbulent times" unless he or she has been the parent of one, two, three, or more teens. I also have a conviction that a person can't write about the ministry of pastoring unless this person has been a pastor. One has little advice to give unless he or she has been there, felt that, done that, and experienced that.

After reading only one page of this book you realize that Bob Broadbooks has been a pastor. He still is a pastor! I'll listen to someone who has walked the road, stayed up half the night to save a marriage, wept with those who weep, laughed with those who laugh. This pastor has something valuable to say to every pastor in the world. He has been there!

The author says a pastor needs to concentrate on three things: people, preaching, and prayer. On the other side of the issue, there are three challenges—yea, four—that can destroy a pastor: the glory, the gold, the girls, and the grind. Every pastor needs to read at least the two chapters that deal with these challenges!

While Bob Broadbooks was and is a pastor, he

is serving as a district superintendent—and has for nearly a decade. But he is a district superintendent with a pastor's heart. Some superintendents have a pastor's heart; some don't. Bob does.

I have known Bob Broadbooks for many years. I was his district superintendent when he and Carol pastored in Lakewood, Colorado. I learned in those days that Pastor Bob reserved one day a month as his "day of solitude." Since that idea and practice resonated with me, I have urged ministers in retreats across the country to schedule one day a month for solitude. This practice will revolutionize and revitalize every pastor's ministry. I was pleased to read about it again in one of Pastor Bob's letters to Pastor Doug. It is a powerful practice.

Being a pastor in the 21st century isn't easy! It's a true challenge. But God still needs pastors to shepherd His people. Clearly, it can be the most rewarding work in the world. If you want to sharpen your ministry skills, read from those who have excelled in the ministry of pastoring. Change the greetings in the letters in this book from "Dear Pastor Doug" to "Dear Pastor (your name)." This book is personal, it is fresh, it is genuine, it is authentic, it makes great sense, it will make you a better pastor or a better friend of a pastor. It is rich!

—James H. Diehl
General Superintendent
Church of the Nazarene

Preface

I was privileged to be called "Pastor Bob" for 20 years. When I arrived at my first ministry assignment, one of the first issues that arose was "What do you want us to call you?"

"Rev. Broadbooks" seemed stuffy for a 25-year-old, so I suggested "Pastor Bob." That was my name for all the years I served in pastoral ministry, and I wore it proudly.

When I began the ministry assignment of district superintendent for my denomination, however, no one called me "Pastor Bob" anymore. I missed that endearing term. I remember distinctly the moment several years later when I was visiting a church I had previously pastored—a lady slipped and called me "Pastor Bob." She caught herself and said, "Oh, excuse me, Dr. Broadbooks!"

"Please don't apologize," I said. "I've missed being 'Pastor Bob'!" Today I can think of no more beautiful title than "Pastor."

My pastorates have given the Broadbooks family great joys—some of them bittersweet—and a host of memories. My family still laughs about the funny things that have happened throughout the years. One of my most embarrassing moments was in a Wednesday night service when I was talking about finding some cigarette butts in the church parking lot. I asked what our reaction should be: "Do we get angry because someone has left that filthy litter on church property? Or should we be glad when we see cigarette butts in the parking lot because someone is coming to seek Christ's help? Praise God! They must feel loved and accepted at our church."

Instead of stopping while I was ahead, I reiterated for emphasis. "And what should our reaction be when we see church butts in the parking lot?" Laughter erupted, and I turned crimson. The service was effectively over at that point, and we dismissed. After church one of the men said, "Pastor Bob, I'm sure I've been called a church butt before, but never to my face." We laugh about it still.

We've also experienced bittersweet moments in the parsonage that have driven us to our knees. We rejoice in those memories also. All four of the Broadbooks clan remember the night we left our second church. As we drove west into a beautiful Kansas sunset after finishing a wedding that was the last official act of my ministry there, there was great sadness in the car. I was weeping, and so was my wife, Carol. I wanted one more look at the church to which we had given six years of our lives. I looked over my shoulder, and there in the backseat, Keely, 11, and Lincoln, 8, were crying too. It's hard to say good-bye to folks you love.

If you're a pastor, I envy you. Whether you're just starting out or have been a pastor for years, you're on a great adventure. I haven't been to the moon, climbed Mt. Everest, or discovered the lost ark. But I just can't imagine that anything compares to the excitement, challenge, and reward of pastoring.

You have the privilege of standing regularly behind a sacred desk and talking about divinity as it relates to humanity. There are times when the anointing comes on you and you hear yourself say things for God that you've never said or thought before. Some moments are so holy you feel like slipping off your shoes in honor of His presence.

You'll be there when a grandmother breathes her last and a baby breathes his or her first. You'll be there when a sinner gulps in the fresh air of salvation and is transformed.

You, my friend, have the honor of being called "Pastor." Hold it tenderly in your heart, and tend it carefully with every skill God gives you. You will be, of all men and women, most blessed.

In this little book I share some simple leadership letters that I wrote to my friend, Doug Wyatt. Doug was my associate pastor for eight years and is presently serving as an effective senior pastor. My prayer is that the concepts will bless and encourage you and that all of us will wear the title "Pastor" with great reverence and respect.

Acknowledgments

I am grateful . . .

for the help of my secretary, Nina Lovell, in preparing the manuscript.

for the encouragement of my friend Karen Dean Fry to write.

for the love and support of my wife, Carol, my daughter, Keely, my son-in-law, Matthew Mullins, and my son, Lincoln

1
Rock Altar Rituals

Dear Pastor Doug,

For some preachers, *ritual* is a bad word. It brings to mind formalism, dry and dusty liturgy, and deadness. But rituals aren't bad. In fact, God uses rituals to help our memories work. He took two very common items, bread and juice, and told us to take them often "in remembrance" of Him. How many times our hearts have been blessed at His table! That ritual is a good thing.

My friend David told me about a beautiful ritual I had to see for myself. In northeast Alabama is a little crossroads called Spring Garden. From the school, go two miles northeast. When you come to the top of the mountain, you'll see a pretty white frame church. It's the Pleasant Arbor Baptist Church, and it's lovely. From the parking lot is a 360-degree view of the whole area.

But the most beautiful site is hidden in the trees behind the church, and it's there that the true strength of Pleasant Arbor resides. There's no sign pointing the way, and there's no need to advertise the location. The people to whom it's special know right where it is. Folks have been coming there for decades.

It's called the Rock Altar. Humanly speaking,

it's not all that beautiful. It's just a pile of rocks about five feet high and about fifteen feet around the base. I don't know exactly when the ritual started, but a long time ago the members of Pleasant Arbor began bringing rocks to that place. Before every Sunday night service and every revival service and just about anytime there arose a serious need, the prayer warriors of Pleasant Arbor brought a rock and gathered to pray.

David said he remembers as a boy, about 50 years ago, walking to church. He could hear them praying, and mixed in with the "amens" was the clinking of rocks as they were thrown one by one onto the pile. David said he's sure there are several rocks in that altar with his name on them.

When I visited Rock Altar, I didn't see names written on any of the stones, but God knows which stones represented prayers for David. If He can collect all the tears of the saints, He can keep track of those stones. I'll tell you what I did see, though. There were some huge rocks on that altar that I'm sure were not carried there by one person. I imagine mom-and-dad teams brought some of the big ones as they came to pray for wayward sons and daughters. I remember seeing a flat rock with five little stones arranged on it in a circle. I can see a mother there, praying, *O God, don't let our circle be broken.*

The rocks aren't especially beautiful. They haven't been washed and shined. But still, it's a beautiful scene. There was a holy hush on that place, permeated by the prayers of those saints that have been offered through the decades. What a thrilling ritual!

Many times when a new pastor comes to a church, he or she says, *We have to change this church, . . . What this church needs is transformation. . . . We're not going to do anything the way it's been done before. . . . We're starting over.* That's a shortsighted approach that won't work. A wise pastor will cherish and honor a church's best traditions and rituals. The church won't follow the new pastor if they're made to feel that nothing in their past is important.

Doug, if you find a rock altar at the church, don't demolish it. Go ahead and throw on a few rocks, and hope and pray there are many rocks thrown in your name. Rituals that are blessed of God are beautiful!

Pleased with the prospects,
BB

P. S. Check out the wisdom of Solomon: "Do not move an ancient boundary stone set up by your forefathers" (Prov. 22:28).

2
Lifesavers

Dear Pastor Doug,

After Ronald Reagan's terms as president of the United States, he returned to California. When he was still receiving visitors, he welcomed them into his office and gladly shared with them his memorabilia. Placed around the office were photographs of great importance to him. As he walked the visitors around the room, he directed the conversation to each of the photos.

Before the ravages of Alzheimer's disease erased his memory, one of the last facts Reagan remembered seemed rather strange. One of the pictures was of himself wearing a swimsuit when he was a young man serving as a lifeguard on the Rock River in Illinois. People often got into trouble while swimming in that river. Reagan was a strong swimmer and aware of the treacherous currents. When he saw someone in trouble, he sprang into action.

Standing by the photo, Reagan asked his visitors, "Do you know how many people I saved from drowning?" And he quickly answered his own question. "Seventy-seven!" It was one fact Reagan remembered long after names, faces, and other precious memories were lost to him.

Strange? Maybe. Maybe not. Saving a life is unforgettable. Ronald Reagan didn't say "around seventy-five" or "almost eighty." He remembered exactly — seventy-seven. Each one counted.

Imagine this. You're walking along a beach down near the water where the sand is smooth. You're intrigued by how quickly the shiny water sinks into the sand. You notice something bobbing in the water far out from shore. Suddenly you realize it's a person. Without thinking, you splash into the water and swim out to help. When you get there, you reach below the surface and snatch the little girl from the water. She's stopped breathing. You struggle as you swim her back to shore and then lay her gently onto the sand. As you push the hair away from her face, you see that her lips are blue, and you can't detect a pulse.

People are beginning to gather. Instinctively you open her mouth and tilt her head back a bit. As you hold her nose, you begin to breathe into her mouth. Your own heart is beating almost uncontrollably, hers not at all. As you breathe into her mouth you pray fervently, *O God, spare her! Spare her!*

After a while, she coughs. Seawater comes. You tilt her head to the side, but you keep breathing into her mouth. You see her chest rise just a little bit, and her lips begin to move. Her eyes flutter. As she sucks in fresh air, her masklike face begins to lose its blueness. As the blood begins to move, her cheeks are turning pink. Suddenly the professionals are there, and they whisk her away.

Did you get a glimpse of the thrill of saving a life? It must be indescribable joy!

Every time you introduce someone to Christ, you're saving a life. You watch as he or she prays and breathes in the fresh air of salvation. Blue, lifeless lives take in the saving blood of Jesus Christ. Blinded eyes flutter open with new sight. Mute lips move, praising God. What a thrill! God uses *you* to save lives. You'll remember the number, because you remember every one. And every single one has a name

I envy you, Doug. You're in the perfect place to see this happen. You'll see it at an altar, a couch, a waiting room, an intensive care unit, a restaurant, and, yes, maybe even on a beach.

You'll see it as often as you want, really. One man said, "The harder I work, the luckier I get." The more times you throw out the lifeline, the more people will be saved. Hey, Doug—stroll those beaches every chance you get!

Pleased with the prospects,
BB

P. S. Doug, check out the wisdom of Solomon: "The fruit of the righteous is a tree of life, and he who wins souls is wise" (Prov. 11:30).

3

Promoter or Pastor

Dear Pastor Doug,

When Nazarene General Superintendent Orville Jenkins ordained me, he placed my ordination parchment in my hand. It seemed he stared straight into my soul as he said, "These elder's orders are clean and unsullied. If by the conduct of your life you ever stain them, I will expect you to return them to us." That night I made sacred vows that, with God's help, I will always keep.

I expect you remember your ordination, too, don't you, Doug? I would guess that moment is burned into the memory of every ordained pastor —as it should be.

A few weeks ago I opened a letter that came to the district office from a preacher friend of mine. My heart sank as I pulled out his ordination certificate and his terse letter. It was just a couple of lines.

He wrote, "I must return my parchment. Please forgive me." Tears stung my eyes. It wasn't just my sorrow and his sorrow. It was every preacher's sorrow.

When any preacher has a lapse, you and I are lessened as well. The honor afforded the ministry through the centuries is diminished when something like this happens, and you and I pay. We are given less respect and fewer hearts will be open to what we say.

My prayer for you and me, Doug, is that we will never dishonor our calling. As I have watched pastors fall, there seems to be a pattern. It seems to me they quit pastoring and started promoting. Without even noticing, they began to build their own little kingdom rather than *the* Kingdom. They prayed and preached and pastored, thinking, *How do I look? Am I sounding good? Maybe this sermon will get me a raise! Perhaps this year of church growth will get me some denominational recognition.* Every action, every thought, every plan is geared toward *promoting.* This isn't what pastoring should be about.

Promoters want to receive. Pastors want to give.

Promoters manipulate people. Pastors motivate people.

Promoters seek to use. Pastors seek to be used.

Promoters ask, "How can the church help me?" Pastors ask, "How can I help the church?

Promoters look at a person to see what that person can do. Pastors look at a person to see who that person is.

Promoters ask, "What can this person do for me?" Pastors ask, "What can I do for this person?"

It's a mind-set, Doug. Check yours regularly.

Pretend it's Monday, and you're parked in front of the home of Sunday morning's visitors ready to go to the door to thank them for coming to church. What are you thinking? *Hey—that's a BMW in the driveway! Man—this house must have cost a fortune! Wow—these people's tithes will be a tidy sum! I'd better smile big and put on the charm.* If that's what you're thinking, you're a promoter.

Or do you find yourself thinking, *I wonder if these people are lonely. Maybe all this stuff isn't meeting their deepest needs and they came to church yesterday for help. O Lord, help me say the right things and show them Your love. Help me minister to their needs.* If that's what you're thinking, you're a pastor. And you're about to be a fruitful pastor.

It's a mind-set, Doug. Check yours regularly.

Pleased with the prospects,

BB

P. S. Hey, Doug—check out the wisdom of Solomon: "The leech has two daughters. 'Give! Give!' they cry" (Prov. 30:15).

4
Norman Is an Island

Dear Pastor Doug,

In recent years a serious accident occurred in Illinois when a train struck a school bus. Hospice nurse Helen Getchell was one of the first to reach the scene. She found a seriously injured boy. He was choking, and Helen yelled frantically for someone to go find something she could use to suction him. When she spoke to reporters later, she explained that somebody ran and got a turkey baster and that she used that to suction the boy.

The nurse didn't know the boy's name, but through the television interview she sent a message to his family. She said, "I want to tell the mother, 'You have a good kid,' because he was breathing. He did what I asked him to do. It just wasn't enough. He died in my arms. That's what I want to tell his mom. He didn't die by himself—I was there, and I held him."

Nurse Getchell realized that it's a very sad thing to die alone, and she thought it would be comforting to this young boy's family to know that she was with him at the end. As sad as it is to die alone, it's even sadder to live alone.

I have a pastor friend named Norman. He's

like a lot of us—busy all the time. Yet Norman's lonely. Many preachers fall into this trap. They're accustomed to filling the role of the caring professional in all situations. The pastor is expected to have all the answers and is expected to meet the needs of all who come to him or her. Many look to their pastors for guidance, solace, encouragement, and hope.

Norman feels alone. He helps others, but who helps him? He doesn't feel comfortable speaking to the district superintendent about his needs. He thinks his leader would be somehow disappointed in him if he knew. He could talk to his wife, but he doesn't want to burden her with too much. She's overwhelmed as it is. So he talks to the Lord, but still he suffers quietly in his loneliness.

Norman is an island. At least he's trying to be. But John Donne was right when he said, "No man is an island unto himself." Norman can't function very well as an island. And neither can you, Doug. You'll need some help with your load. Never be ashamed about that need. Open up to a fellow pastor—even a pastor from another denomination. That's OK. Always feel free to come to me. Some things just need to be talked through and then become clearer once they're verbalized. Find a prayer partner, and encourage each other.

John Wesley said, "There's no such thing as solitary religion." Doug, there's no such thing as solitary pastoring. The calling is too big, too heavy, and too demanding to go it alone. Norman is trying to be an island, but he can't. I don't think anybody can. I don't think anybody needs to.

It's the nature of humanity to need the help and hope that other people can give. I read about a 15-year-old boy named Doug who was admitted to the hospital with a temperature of 105 degrees. They discovered that he had leukemia, plus he had developed pneumonia. For 10 days his mother stayed with him in his hospital room. The doctors told him that he would undergo chemotherapy, would go bald, and would probably struggle. Doug was smart enough to know that leukemia could be fatal.

One day he opened his eyes, looked around the room, and said, "Mother, I thought that when you're in the hospital you get flowers."

His aunt overheard this and called in an order to the local flower shop. The young woman who answered the phone at the flower shop took the order. The aunt said, "I want the planter to be especially attractive. It's for my teenage nephew who has leukemia." The salesclerk took down the information.

When the arrangement arrived at Doug's room, he opened the envelope and read the card from his aunt. Then he noticed another card tucked away in the flowers. He opened it and read, "Doug, I took the order from your aunt. I work at the flower shop. I had leukemia when I was seven years old. I'm 22 years old now. Good luck! My heart goes out to you. Sincerely, Laura Bradley."

For the first time since entering the hospital, Doug brightened up. He had talked with a lot of doctors and nurses since his diagnosis, but this card was the first indication that he could beat the disease. Doug's family sought out Laura to thank her for writing the card and including it with the flowers. She said, "It reminded me of when I first got leukemia, and I wanted him to know that he really could get better. I didn't tell anyone about writing the card, because I was afraid I might get in trouble."

Isn't it interesting that Doug was in a hospital filled with millions of dollars' worth of sophisticated medical equipment and was surrounded by excellent doctors and nurses—but it was a quickly written note from a salesclerk at the flower shop that gave him real hope? He received a word of encouragement from someone who had walked the same path he was walking.

Fifteen-year-old boys need words of hope. And so do pastors. Isolation eventually takes its toll. Norman needs a brother, and so do you, Doug.

Hey, Doug—the boat is sailing. You have permission to leave your island!

Pleased with the prospects,
BB

P. S. Hey, Doug—check out the wisdom of Solomon: "He who trusts in himself is a fool, but he who walks in wisdom is kept safe" (Prov. 28:26).

5

The White Flag of Surrender

Dear Pastor Doug,

"These people don't listen to me anymore. I can't get them to do anything."

When I hear these words from a pastor, I know it's the beginning of the end of his or her pastoral stay. That pastor will soon be looking for the exit.

If such pastors honestly look inside, they might discover the reasons the congregation is not listening anymore. They have no doubt done all they know to do and have tried excruciatingly hard to move the church forward, but it hasn't happened. So they end up waving the white flag of surrender.

Doug, if you ever get to that point, I suggest that you listen to the tapes of your messages for the past several months. Have you developed an angry tone of voice? People tend to quit listening when you speak *at* them with demanding, condescending words. They can detect it when you cease loving them and their church.

But you can get that love back. You can go to your prayer closet and weep your way back to joy. You can turn in your white flag of surrender, and

God can replace it with a beautiful banner of love. The "banner of love" imagery comes from the Song of Solomon. Evidently a lover invited his special mate into a big banquet hall for a meal. There he had posted a banner of love over that special someone. Of course, many people see that passage as referring to our relationship with God. As we enter into the banquet hall of rich fellowship with the Lord, He can dramatically transform our outlook. A new love can be rekindled.

Soon you'll discover that your preaching is improving. Instead of telling them to *do* something, you'll challenge yourself and them to *be* something. You'll stop emphasizing *doing* and will help them thirst for *being* more like Christ. When they're assured that you love them and that you would give yourself sacrificially for them, they'll follow you anywhere God leads.

So, Doug, if you ever feel like saying, "They don't listen to me anymore," it's not time to resign—it's time to pray. The lyrics of this song say it well:

Weep Your Way to Joy

It's amazing how it happens
  You bring your heart so full of pain.
You pray and keep on praying;
  And soon your joy returns again.

When your sin begins to trap you,
  And your life has lost control,

You don't have to stay frustrated.
   There is One who heals the soul.

Are you tired and heavy-hearted;
   Not sure if you should go or stay?
Just hang on a little longer
   And quickly find a place to pray.

Weep your way to joy.
   The Spirit's power employ.
At an altar of prayer,
You can meet Jesus there,
   And weep your way to joy.
                    —Bob Broadbooks
                    Pleased with the prospects,
                    BB

P. S. Hey, Doug—check out the wisdom of Solomon: "He has taken me to the banquet hall, and his banner over me is love" (Song of Solomon 2:4).

6

"I'm Overwhelmed!"

Dear Pastor Doug,

It's not unusual for a young pastor to feel overwhelmed as he or she begins a pastorate. There's so much to be concerned about in pastoring a church: programs to oversee for youth, children, and adults; concern for Sunday School, missions, the building and grounds, the finances, hospital calls, and emergencies in the lives of the parishioners. The workload is heavy.

There are three areas on which a pastor can concentrate to help things fall into place: the people, the preaching, and prayer. It's a good thing for you to study church growth principles, counseling techniques, and the latest business practices that can be applied to the church. But if you spread yourself too thin, your energies will be too widely diffused. If you concentrate on people, preaching, and prayer, you'll be effective, and your ministry will flourish.

Yogi Berra said, "Ninety percent of baseball is mental; the other half is physical." Applying that laughable logic to ministry, let's say that 90 percent of being a pastor is dealing with people and the other half is everything else. God gifts some

31

people with the natural ability to get along with all types of people. But everyone can improve.

I met a pastor the other day who wanted to argue about everything I said. The scowl on his face looked permanent. It didn't surprise me to hear that his church is struggling. Instead of being drawn to him, people flee from him. But remember, Doug, that you can love people, study people, and put yourself in their shoes, and your church will grow.

Concentrate on your preaching. If you have something to say and you say it well, people will come and listen. Immerse yourself in the study of communication. Make the study of preaching your hobby, and always be on the lookout for a good story or an interesting phrase—and then write it down. You may think it's unforgettable today, but—trust me on this—in a few days you won't remember it. So write it down. Read the Bible and the newspaper every day. People want to be fed, and if they can't get a good meal at your table, there are plenty of other restaurants in town.

And most important, concentrate on prayer. This is the most important work you do. Unfortunately, many preachers leave it until last. My challenge to you is to read E. M. Bounds's *The Power of Prayer* every year. It will drive you to your knees.

Be an example in private prayer. Many times when problems crop up in the church, our first thought is to go and fix it. Resist that temptation, and take it to God. He may tell you to do nothing about it, or He may give you a plan of action that would not have crossed your mind. But pray first!

Henri Nouwen says that the life of ministry is like a wheel with a hub. We pastors often run around the rim trying to reach everybody, but it's best to live in the hub of prayer. We'll still be connected to everybody, but we won't have to run so fast.

Be an example in corporate prayer. Call the church together to pray. Have a real prayer meeting. Don't preach—just sing and pray. Call out to God!

There's an old saying that holds true today: "You can tell how popular a church is by who comes on Sunday morning. You can tell how popular the preacher is by who comes on Sunday night. But you can tell how popular Jesus is by who comes to prayer meeting." Your effectiveness as a pastor will increase dramatically as you pray and lead your church to pray.

Many pastors get caught in the stressful trap of keeping programs going. There's nothing wrong with programs—the church needs them. But put your major effort into the ministry of people, preaching, and prayer. Then your church will move forward.

Pleased with the prospects,
BB

P. S. Hey, Doug—check out the wisdom of Solomon: "The prayer of the upright is his delight" (Prov. 15:8, KJV).

7

Medicine for Dry Bones

Dear Pastor Doug,

Carol and I were driving down a country road the other day and came upon a dilapidated little church. You wouldn't believe the name on the sign: "Little Hope Primitive Baptist Church." Now if I were going to name a church, I think that "Little Hope" would be about the last name on my list. It doesn't do much to inspire excitement for the future. But unfortunately we sometimes act as if that were our church's name. Pastors must never give in to the temptation to lose hope for their churches.

I know the denominational manual says we should have a board meeting every month, but there were some months I just didn't want to go. Can you identify? Maybe the statistics weren't the best, and I knew the board members would point it out. "Oh, look, Pastor—Sunday School attendance is down." "Did you notice that we spent more than we took in? If we keep doing that, we'll be out of business." "Pastor, the teens didn't clean up the van after their last trip." "We're two months behind on our budget payments, Pastor."

Board meetings like that made me cringe. When it happens to you, Doug—and it will—

force yourself to remain calm. If they see panic in your eyes or hear it in your voice, their confidence will be shaken. They'll begin to worry. If they know you're shaken, they'll begin to think, *Maybe this is serious. We really are in danger!* But if they see you calmly confident in the face of all the comments, they'll remain calm also. Reply with "Yes, this hasn't been our best month in Sunday School, but God's going to help us. We're starting a new class, and that's going to increase our attendance. There are some good signs in our receipts. Let's keep praying that God will make us generous people." In the face of each negative comment, preach positives.

This attitude will help when dealing with people problems, too. I remember counseling with a man who was really struggling. He had just lost his job, his wife, and his mother. It was a real Job story. As he finished telling me of his losses, I felt a multitude of emotions—sorrow, pain, disappointment, helplessness, and frustration. But you know what I said? Certainly not what I was feeling. I spoke with positive faith. I said, "I don't know why. I don't know how or when, but I do know this—God is going to help you through this. He's a great God, and He's ultimately in control. He'll see you through it." I didn't feel that—I *knew* that.

Doug, you're a dispenser of hope and positive faith. Folks can find someone to commiserate with them just about anywhere, but there are very few of you around. You must spout faith even though deep inside you wonder how in the world God is ever going to fix this! You're convinced that He is "able to do exceeding abundantly above all that we ask or think" (Eph. 3:20, KJV).

Be positive every chance you get, and soon the church will sound just like you.

Pleased with the prospects,
BB

P. S. Hey, Doug—consider the wisdom of Solomon: "A joyful heart is good medicine, But a broken spirit dries up the bones" (Prov. 17:22, NASB).

8
Church Fights

Dear Pastor Doug,

So far, God has spared you from having to referee a spat at church. But you may not always be so fortunate. Just in case, you should probably save this letter for future reference. Chances are you'll need it. I have two pieces of advice, each 2,500 years old.

My son, Lincoln, introduced me to the writing of Sun Tzu. He was a great Chinese general who wrote a book called *The Art of War* in the sixth century B.C. It's interesting reading that's studied today by military and business people.

Sun Tzu taught that sometimes retreat is a good thing. If you're going to have too many casualties and if the prize for winning is not that significant, retreat is honorable. It's the old story of "you may win the battle but lose the war."

I know some pastors who have to "win" every time. Their egos are so gargantuan that they can't step back from a tussle. Late Nazarene general superintendent Hardy C. Powers used to say, "If I'm going to spill my blood, it's going to be for something important." I'm afraid many pastors spill their blood over insignificant issues, and then when something of consequence comes up, they have no blood left. As Sun Tzu said, retreat might be the wise course of action. You can get your way over what color to paint the bathrooms if you want to, but I think a man or woman ought to save some of his or her blood — or influence — for a more important debate.

The wise pastor knows the difference between perishable and cherishable. There are some things that he or she should go to the mat for, but there are other things that are just not as important. Allow the unimportant things to perish. If the pastor can't tell the difference, his or her ministry might perish.

A number of years ago a pastor began his ministry at a church and discovered that they were not using the denominational hymnal. Instead, they had "shaped-note" hymnals. He pushed through the purchasing of new hymnals and took it upon himself to remove the "shaped-note" hymnals from the racks and stored them away. When the denominational leader came for an annual visit, the pastor was very proud of the fact that he had finally gotten the church to make this momentous change. Soon after that, the pastor's vote was held. When the tally came back, he had received a unanimous vote — everyone had voted "no." The pastor's ministry perished because he didn't know the difference between cherishable and perishable.

Another fascinating thing that Sun Tzu said was that when you're surrounding your adversaries, you should always leave them a back door of escape. If your adversary knows there's no chance of escape, he or she will fight harder. If your adversary knows that death is imminent, his or her fighting will be fiercer, deciding, "I'm going to die anyway, so I'm taking as many with me as I can." But if the person knows there's no way to win but there's a chance of escape, he or she will cease the fight and slip away. Doug, if you back people into a corner, they'll begin to claw. Give them a way out. Be conciliatory. Offer a compromise. There will be less carnage in the end, and the church will continue on.

Pray often for wisdom, Doug. God will tell you what to do. Sun Tzu said, "Therefore, just as water retains no constant shape, so in warfare there are no constant conditions. He who can modify his tactics in relation to his opponent and thereby succeed in winning may be called a heaven-born captain." Doug, you're a "heaven-born captain." Your wisdom is from above. The Lord will tell you what to do in that church fight. It may be to retreat, or it may be to provide a way of escape for your adversary. Listen carefully and prayerfully to our "heavenly General."

Pleased with the prospects,
BB

P. S. Hey, Doug—check out the wisdom of Solomon: "The beginning of strife is like letting out water, So abandon the quarrel before it breaks out" (Prov. 17:14, NASB).

9

Tuned-out Trumpets

Dear Pastor Doug,

The Muslims in North America are confused these days about where to face during prayer. Muslims pray five times each day by turning toward Mecca, Saudi Arabia. Some here in the United States and Canada favor turning southeast, the straightest route on a flat map. Many more prefer facing the northeast, which is the shortest route on the globe. The issue has divided North American Muslims greatly. It's the simple things that often divide us.

I'm thankful that I can face any direction I want to when I pray. Most of the time I face up.

It's pretty easy to confuse a congregation. Preachers do it frequently. They attend a conference or seminar and come home the next Sunday to announce a new discipleship program. The next month, they'll explain to the congregation that a new calling program will start. The next month they read a book, and suddenly there's another new idea to be implemented. The congregation never hears any more about any of these new programs, and they never go any further. There's no follow-through. The folks get confused and skeptical. Soon they stop listening to "Pastor's big ideas."

Doug, I urge you to move slowly. You'll feel pressure to act and make decisions, but weigh the consequences. Don't rush decisions, and don't make pronouncements to the church before you make adequate preparation. Abraham Lincoln said, "Nothing valuable can be lost by taking time." If it's the right thing to do, it will still be available to you after you've considered it fully and prayed about it sufficiently.

In *The Complete Art of War* (translated by Ralph D. Sawyer, Westview Press, 1996) Sun Tzu wrote, "When the general is weak and without authority, when his orders are not clear and distinct, when there are no fixed duties assigned to officers and men, and the ranks are found in a slovenly, haphazard manner, the result is utter disorganization." The people of the church can't follow an uncertain trumpet. When the directions are not clear, people get nervous. When you change your tune all the time, the symphony stops.

When this happens, you cease being the leader. People in the congregation who are natural leaders begin to gather their followers. Soon your church is divided. If the person in charge of the young people is a natural leader, the youth group will begin to take over direction of the church. If the natural leader is in the music program, the music program begins to run the church. This could happen in the children's program, the sports program, or any other area of the church. Natural leaders rise to the surface if there is a vacuum in pastoral leadership. Then, instead of one trumpet leading the congregation, you suddenly have ten little cornets blaring, and the forward progress of the church stalls. The church is divided.

You might ask me, "Have you always known what direction to lead your church?" Let me answer that question with a story from the life of Daniel Boone. He was asked, "Have you ever been lost in the wilderness?"

Boone replied, "No, but I've been bewildered for three days."

I can identify with that. I didn't always know in which direction to lead the church, but when that happened I didn't pretend that I did. I spent extended times in prayer until I had clear direction from the Lord.

Move slowly, but move deliberately. Abe Lincoln said, "I'm a slow walker, but I never walk backward." Moving slowly is not so bad—just be sure to move.

Pleased with the prospects,
BB

P. S. Hey, Doug—check out the wisdom of Solomon: "Do you see a man who is hasty in his words? There is more hope for a fool than for him" (Prov. 29:20, NASB).

10

Every Paul Needs a Timothy

Dear Pastor Doug,

If someone in your church declares this year that God has called him or her into full-time ministry, rejoice! The annual report may not reflect this success, but you just had a great year. God has entrusted you with a beautiful responsibility. You are now a Paul, and you have a Timothy.

When I told my pastor that God wanted me to be a preacher, he leaped into action. He made sure I was at the zone rallies. If a missionary or an evangelist preached anywhere nearby, he took me there. He carted me all over Nebraska to make sure I was at the teen camps and assemblies. Even if I was the only teenager from our church going, he got me there. He gave me opportunities to pray and preach. I went calling with him. I became his project. When it was time for me to go to college, he gently nudged me toward one affiliated with our denomination. It didn't hurt that when the college president was in town, the preacher and my parents had him over to our house for ice cream and cake. I still have the picture of President Curt Smith and me at our dining room table. I think all of it was a plot, but I'm grateful they cared.

I think our temptation today is to let our institutions of higher education be responsible. A young person feels a call, and our only response is "You had better plan to go to a Christian college." But, Doug, the process should begin at home.

When Jesus was training His disciples, He did not immediately start looking for a Christian college for them to attend. He spent time with them, and they went with Him everywhere. Doug, if your phone rings and you discover that someone from your congregation is being admitted to the hospital, don't go alone. Call up your Timothy and say you'll be right there to pick him or her up for a visit to the hospital. It's called "on-the-job training."

Jesus was in constant contact with His Heavenly Father. The Bible shows us that He often went away to spend time in prayer. Since His disciples were often with Him, they saw Him going to prayer. It was good for them to see firsthand the way their Master approached His ministry.

Jesus taught that in order to be a leader, one must be a servant. He modeled servanthood to His disciples as He touched everyone who came to Him. Your Timothy needs to develop your spirit of servanthood. He or she will not catch that spirit if all he or she sees you doing is preaching your Sunday morning sermon. Make sure your Timothy spends time with you.

In spending time with Jesus, the disciples were able to watch Him in different situations. When

He was under pressure, they saw how He controlled His frustration. When He was tired, they saw what He did. They saw that nothing distracted Him from His mission to bring the Kingdom to this world.

Not only can you mentor the nuts and bolts of the ministry, but also by spending time with you, your Timothy can catch the spirit of your ministry.

When God gives you a Timothy, begin to mentor him or her. Teach the concepts that are important to you. It will be enjoyable, and you'll be doing exactly what Jesus did.

Pleased with the prospects,
BB

P. S. Hey, Doug—check out the wisdom of Solomon: "Do not withhold good from those to whom it is due, When it is in your power to do it" (Prov. 3:27, NASB).

11

If It Runs You,
It Ruins You

Dear Pastor Doug,

I remember the first time my young son, Lincoln, went with me to an automatic car wash. He was sitting on the armrest next to me. (Children's safety seats were not yet in vogue.) Our car was pulled into the bay and lurched to a stop. The spray hit the car, and soon the gigantic brushes were coming at us from all directions. The noise got louder and louder. Lincoln's eyes got bigger and bigger. He let out a loud scream, threw his arms around my neck, and buried his face against my cheek. He held on for dear life until the carwash ordeal was over.

Lincoln was afraid because he didn't understand. It was just a bath for the car, but he didn't know that. Worry about the unknown often causes great anxiety.

Doug, I'm a little concerned about you. You've been working awfully hard. It seems you've been thinking, *I have to make this church grow. My future depends on it. It's all on my shoulders. I have to do it all myself.* You're experiencing moments of fear and anxiety. I can see it in you because I saw it in me.

The self-imposed pressure was so great in my

first church that I found myself awakened each night with a burning stomach and the need for a glass of milk. I remember that we were in the middle of a building program. I was worrying about a myriad of details, many of which were unfamiliar territory for me, and the fear was catching up with me.

If fear and worry run your life, they will ruin your life. But if you let faith run your life, it will release you. Fear and worry make miserable life partners.

Marcus Aurelius was a great philosopher who ruled the Roman Empire. He uttered these life-changing words: "Our life is what our thoughts make it." You can control your thoughts. Whatever you allow yourself to think will form your life. The writer of Proverbs said the same thing: "As he thinks in his heart, so is he" (23:7, NKJV). Abraham Lincoln chimed, "Most folks are about as happy as they make up their minds to be."

There's another old saying that applies: "Fear is the darkroom where you develop your negatives." It's so easy to operate with a negative point of view. You think, *Oh, no—the church is about to collapse. I'm not a very good pastor. Others are doing so much more, and they're doing it so much better.* Force those thoughts from your brain, and concentrate on the fact that this is God's church. He is "large and in charge." You don't have to be worried about being "successful." All you have to do is concentrate on doing your best and being faithful.

Relax and be happy in Him. You can make up your mind that you're not going to worry!

Listen to the testimony of a great Methodist missionary:

Fifty-two years ago I knelt before a chair with a letter spread out before me — a letter from a mission board secretary, asking me to go to India. I knew that the way I answered that letter might determine my life work. So I prayed: "Dear Lord, I'm willing to go anywhere, do anything, and be anything You want me to be, provided You show me where." The Inner Voice replied, "It's India." I arose from my knees and repeated those words to myself: "It's India." It was settled. I was called to be a missionary. Fifty-one years later I knelt in that same room before a chair, probably not the same one, and thanked God with a deep heartfelt thanks for the unfolding purpose of these glorious years as a missionary. Success or failure mattered little — being true to that call was the only thing that mattered.

— E. Stanley Jones, *In Christ*

Doug, read that last line again: "Success or failure mattered little — being true to that call was the only thing that mattered."

It's up to you, Doug. It's either "Pass me another glass of milk" or "Pass me not, O gentle Savior." You decide.

Pleased with the prospects,
BB

P. S. Hey, Doug—check out the wisdom of Solomon: "Like a city that is broken into and without walls Is a man who has no control over his spirit" (Prov. 25:28, NASB).

12

Favoritism

Dear Pastor Doug,

Do you remember when Carol and I met you in the church parking lot a few years ago? Your daughter, McKenna, was about two and a half years old. She came running over to us, and I scooped her up. She gave me a big hug around my neck, and we traded kisses. Then she was down and back over to Mom and Dad.

It was a beautiful moment in my life. I soon learned it was a beautiful moment for McKenna, too. You told me later that when McKenna saw us drive into the parking lot, she said, "Pastor Bob's gonna love seeing me!"

She was right, of course. I always love seeing her. I'm glad she senses my love and acceptance and feels free to enter my world. I wish all of us could be as confident as she is.

Unfortunately, for many of us, the older we get the less lovely we see ourselves. We carry around shame and guilt, and we tend to second-guess our worthiness. We wonder how anyone could love to meet us in the church parking lot, so instead of running into waiting arms, we wait alone or run away.

You know what I wish, Doug? I wish that

everyone who thinks about entering one of our churches would feel like McKenna. I wish that everyone felt such love and acceptance there that when it came time for church, instead of thinking, *Nobody's gonna miss me if I don't go today* they would think, *They're gonna love seeing me!* I wish each one would think, *They know how to love a person over there. I need to be there. I want to be there.* Maybe I'm just dreaming. Then again, maybe not.

Doug, your challenge as a pastor is to make every single person feel like McKenna. But too many pastors make the mistake of spending an inordinate amount of time with just a few people in their churches. They go out to lunch with the same people every week. They spend their free time with the members to whom they feel the closest. Other members of the congregation notice; it's obvious to them. And it's a big deal.

They begin to feel left out. They think that only the pastor's friends have his or her ear. Soon there develops a division between the "in crowd" and the "out crowd." Guard yourself against showing any hint of favoritism.

Mothers are good at this. I have an older brother and sister, but I'm certain that my mother loves me best. I'm also certain that my brother, Roy, and my sister, Anita, think that each of them is Mom's favorite. Mothers know how to make each child feel special. Pastors need the same ability with their parishioners.

I challenge you, Doug, to love them all the

same. In prayer, God can give you a deep love for all your people. You'll be amazed at what He does. Someone will come to you and say something negative about one of your parishioners. Your first thought will be, *Well, you don't know her like I know her. She's not at all like that. She's one of the best people in the world.*

Pray, Doug. Pray. God will increase your love for your people. You see, Doug, it's the only fair thing to do, because your people have been doing the same thing. They've been praying that God would help them to love you. I wouldn't venture to guess for whom it has been more challenging — you or them!

Pleased with the prospects,
BB

P. S. Hey, Doug — check out the wisdom of Solomon: "To show partiality is not good" (Prov. 28:21).

13

How to Destroy a Preacher

Dear Pastor Doug,

An American proverb states, "There are three things that can destroy a preacher—the glory, the gold, and the girls." That's certainly true, but I can think of another one—*the grind*.

Unless you've pastored a church, it would be hard to comprehend how difficult it can be. You must stay fresh while preaching challenging, inspirational messages several times a week. You're on call 24 hours a day. You must be available when there are tragedies, disagreements, hurt feelings, and pain. Many of your congregation will expect you to be a miracle worker. The challenge is significant, and it can be a grind. Doug, this is why it's so important for you to be religious about taking your day off.

Many years ago Lord Moran wrote a book called *Anatomy of Courage,* a classic study of the soldier's struggle against fear. He wrote that every soldier has limited amounts of courage, and courage is his capital. He can use it, lose it, and replenish it. He makes withdrawals from the bank of his courage when he's on the front line, and periodically he must step away from the battle to build his capital back up. Even the bravest, most courageous soldiers can crack on the front lines. Their courage must be replenished during leave.

Doug, you're on the front lines. You're a major player in the battle between good and evil, darkness and light. You have limited amounts of courage capital available. Glory, gold, and girls can destroy; but so can the spending of all your courage.

Be sure to take a day off. Gandhi, the great leader of India, took one day a week for thought and prayer. He found that if he did not, he lost mental freshness and spiritual power and was in danger of becoming formal, mechanical, and losing his vitality.

That describes many preachers—no mental freshness, no spiritual power; formal, mechanical, and without vitality. They've spent all their courage capital. On your day off do something you enjoy. Every person needs a hobby. Evangelist Bob Hoots kept telling me that it was important for me to collect something, that it would be a healthy diversion. Finally, when I turned 45, I found something to collect. Starting with a milk bottle from my hometown, I decided to collect one from every state. I thought it was an original idea. Later on, I discovered that many people do the same thing. Now I have a milk bottle from every state, plus another 250. Men are naturally hunters and gatherers. There's something refreshing about hunting for articles that interest you. I'm not suggesting that you spend every one of your days off enjoying your hobby; but you need regular time away from the grind to replenish your courage.

While pastoring, I enjoyed a day of solitude once a month. It was a wonderful experience for my soul. In January I marked those 12 days on my calendar and guarded them jealously. When one of those days rolled around, I was out of the office and away from the house. I spent my days of solitude in many different places—in my car overlooking a lake, on a mountain, and at the beach. I took just my Bible, hymnal, and church directory. During the day, I fasted lunch, sang, prayed, read, and thought. I interceded for everyone in the church. At the end of the day I discovered that I had banked more courage for the next challenge.

Courage is not something we're all born with. And we don't gain courage due to the absence of difficult circumstances in our lives. It doesn't come just because we're having a restful day. It's something that's provided by God himself. You can actually request and receive it from His hand.

When the disciples were caught in a storm while trying to cross the lake, Jesus said to them, "Take courage! It is I. Don't be afraid" (Matt. 14:27).

In Acts 23 the apostle Paul had just spoken to the Sanhedrin. It was a stressful event for him. Verse 11 says, "The following night the Lord stood near Paul and said, 'Take courage! As you have testified about me in Jerusalem, so you must also testify in Rome.'"

In both of these verses the Lord said to harried

and harassed people, "Take courage." Notice that He didn't say, "Be courageous." Rather, He said, "Take courage." He's providing it. Doug, you can take Christ's courage. On your weekly day off, during your monthly day of solitude, and any other moment you can steal with Him, you can receive courage.

I suppose the gold, the glory, and the girls have destroyed many preachers—but I suspect many more have been destroyed by the grind.

Don't let the grind get you. Take courage from Christ!

Pleased with the prospects,
BB

P. S. Hey, Doug—check out the wisdom of Solomon: "Blessed is the man who listens to me, Watching daily at my gates, Waiting at my doorposts. For he who finds me finds life And obtains favor from the LORD" (Prov. 8:34-35, NASB).

14
Personal, Not Professional

Dear Pastor Doug,

So here you are about to officiate at your first funeral. God has been gracious to you. Be thankful that your first funeral isn't a suicide, a child, or a family killed in a car accident. Yours is the funeral for an elderly saint. She lived a long and Christlike life. Her funeral will be the celebration of a grand homecoming.

Doug, if pastors aren't careful, they can get into the habit of performing professional funerals. They say all the right things about death in their sermons—the same sermons they give at all their funerals. They read the same Scripture passages—one from the Old Testament and one from the New. The only differences in the funerals they preach are the obituaries.

But if you're willing to make the effort, Doug, you can make each funeral personal. When you get news that someone in your congregation has died, make an appointment to visit with the family. While you're there, ask some key questions. "Did your loved one have any favorite Scriptures?" If so, incorporate them into the service. "What special memories do you have of your loved one?" Try to give them opportunity to talk about events, attributes, and qualities. These tearful interview times can be beautiful moments of celebration and healing.

I remember when Etta Fahrney died. Her grown children had so many memories to share. They told that when they were growing up, their family had lived two miles east of town on a farm. While in grade school the kids walked to and from school. They vividly remembered—now some 50 years later—that there was a big tree stump right next to the road. Every day, Etta stood on that stump, shading her eyes with her hand, peering down the road to make sure they got home safely. Etta watched them all the way.

When they told me that story in the interview, I knew immediately how I wanted to end that funeral. I told the story and then I said, "In my mind's eye, I think I can see Etta standing on another stump watching another highway. It's the highway to heaven, and your mother and grandmother is waiting and watching for all of you to get there, too. She wants to make sure you get home to heaven safely. The good news is—you can make it, too!"

Two years later when Etta's husband, Walter, passed away, we gathered for the funeral. Toward the end of the message I started to mention Etta and the tree stump. The family knowingly smiled at what I was about to say. I suggested that now Walter had joined Etta in the heavenly watch. Arm in arm they were standing on that stump near the heavenly highway. Together again, the Fahrneys wait for their loved ones to make the journey successfully.

Doug, I know that touched the members of the Fahrney family. It was my chance to gently re-mind all of them that their heritage was pointing them to heaven. It was up to them to choose heav-en so that in the end the whole clan would be to-gether again. I think Etta and Walter were pleased.

Hey Doug, get personal at your first funeral.

Pleased with the prospects,

BB

P. S. Hey, Doug—check out the wisdom of Solo-mon: "Like apples of gold in settings of silver Is a word spoken in right circumstances" (Prov. 25:11, NASB).

15

Bennies and Babies

Dear Pastor Doug,

Every pastor dreams of pastoring a loving church. But loving churches don't just happen—they're grown. God can use you to make the churches you pastor loving.

Here's how. Your parishioners are watching you. As they see you treating people tenderly, they begin to do the same. If they see that you have patience with people, they become more patient. When you talk to a child, kneel down and look him or her in the face. If you model the fact that you love all people, the church will also.

Benny just showed up one Sunday morning at a church service, and he kept coming back. He wore the same clothes every Sunday—blue bib overalls and a white T-shirt. He had a speech impediment, and I was unable to understand his name. I asked him what his name was, and he mumbled something that sounded like "Benny." After a few Sundays of me calling him Benny, he tried again to get me to understand his name. I realized finally that he was saying his name was Jack, as in Jack Benny. By that time, though, we were all comfortable calling him Benny, so we just kept calling him that.

Benny loved to come to our church. He always went to the Sunday School class that was serving the best refreshments. Then he waited until everyone left the classroom, and if there was any coffee cake left, he took it with him into the sanctuary. He sat near the front, and while I preached he ate the rest of the coffee cake. It was disconcerting at first, but we eventually got used to it.

After a few weeks, when the altar call was given, Benny made his way to the altar, weeping. The people of our church gathered around him and prayed for him as if he were the most important man in the whole city. And to them he was. They gave time to him and loved him.

On our last Sunday in that church, Benny brought his camera and asked if he could take our picture. Carol and I went out to the front of the building. Benny carefully studied where the sun was to be sure that it was in our faces. Then he aimed the camera at us. Realizing that things weren't quite right, he took a few steps back, aimed it again, stepped a little farther back, and aimed the camera again. We stood there for some time in the hot sun while he prepared to take the picture. Finally he snapped the camera. Then with tears he hugged us and said, "You know, next time you come back, I'm gonna have some film in my camera, and I'm gonna take a *real* picture of you." He cried, we cried, and we laughed together. It was his way of saying, "I love you, and if I had some film and I could take a picture, it would be of you."

I believe that because Carol and I gave our love and our time to Benny, the people in our church took our lead. They relaxed and loved him, too. It's a beautiful thing to pastor a loving church. People are looking for a church like that. You can build one, Doug. It's in you!

Pleased with the prospects,
BB

P. S. Hey, Doug—check out the wisdom of Solomon: "The righteous is concerned for the rights of the poor, The wicked does not understand such concern" (Prov. 29:7, NASB).

16

Bully Pulpit

Dear Pastor Doug,

While pastoring in Denver, I discovered an advertisement in the newspaper saying that the National Convention for Atheists was being held downtown. I wanted to see what that was all about, so I made plans to be there for the opening meeting. I found the hotel where the atheists were gathering and was directed to the meeting room. I sat down and waited for the program to begin. I knew that Madalyn Murray O'Hair was scheduled to speak. When it came time for the meeting to begin, I looked around and counted the number of people in attendance. It didn't take long. The National Convention for Atheists had attracted the huge sum of 30 people from around the country. When I realized so few were there, I said, "Praise the Lord!"

When it came time for Mrs. O'Hair to speak, she pounded the pulpit, made fun of Christians, and berated them sarcastically. She seemed to be a bully. I'm not sure if females can actually qualify as bullies, but I do know this—bullies don't gather a crowd.

We sometimes hear news commentators talk about the president of the United States having the advantage of the "bully pulpit." That phrase originated with President Theodore Roosevelt in the early 1900s when he called the White House "the bully pulpit." It was a terrific platform to persuasively advocate his agenda. Teddy convinced Congress to buy him a train, and he traveled all over the country preaching his agenda. His bully pulpit gave him great power.

Teddy Roosevelt's bully pulpit was a train. Later, Franklin Roosevelt used the radio as his. Ronald Reagan mastered the art of using the television as his bully pulpit.

Doug, pastors need to be careful not to make the Sunday morning service their bully pulpits. They have the microphone, and they can advance either a positive agenda or a negative one. Some preachers just can't handle that much power. They seem to preach with clubs in their hands, and they want to beat their agendas into the congregation.

I've known preachers to read a Scripture, give their interpretation of it, and then comment, "I didn't say that. God did. Don't blame me." That's unfair use of the pulpit.

Some preachers love to say, "God told me to tell you this." This always makes people uncomfortable, because who wants to dispute God? I would use that claim sparingly, Doug. Then, if God does tell you something, it will mean much more when you do say it. When Jesus preached, He didn't beat up on people. As He looked over Jerusalem, He was moved with compassion. The impression I get of Jesus as a preacher is that He didn't speak down to people. He loved them. It was obvious that He cared.

A preacher friend of mine heard a tragic thing in a district assembly he attended. When a pastor stood to give his report, he simply said, "I don't love my people anymore—I'm going to move to another church." The pastor was right about one thing: if you don't love your people anymore, you can't stay.

If a preacher's love for his or her people begins to wane, his or her words will take on the tone of a bully. People sense it. They feel coerced, not loved. If they do what the pastor wants, they do it grudgingly. There isn't much future in the pastor-people relationship.

Remember, Doug—when you preach, don't use a club. Lay it down and let the tears flow. You'll get a whole lot more accomplished.

Pleased with the prospects,
BB

P. S. Hey, Doug—check out the wisdom of Solomon: "He who guards his mouth and his tongue, Guards his soul from troubles. 'Proud,' 'Haughty,' 'Scoffer,' are his names, Who acts with insolent pride" (Prov. 21:23-24, NASB).

17

Whose Side Are You On?

Dear Pastor Doug,

One of your responsibilities as pastor is to anticipate issues that could divide your church. A wise pastor recognizes those things and works to keep them out of the church. Satan loves to divide us, because then the church is impotent. Once a congregation is divided, it stops winning people to the Lord, and the atmosphere is cold, critical, and complaining. A divided church is not a winsome, attractive church. A divided church is on its deathbed. It's critical that the pastor foster unity among his or her people.

People tend to take sides in a church fight, and they're certain they've taken the right side. But anytime a person takes a side in a church fight, he or she ends up being wrong. It isn't intentional. That person believes a principle is involved, but soon the principle becomes a bias, and then the bias becomes an attitude. Satan is good at using good people to divide the church.

The wise church member is not on "the pastor's side" or on "the side opposed to the pastor"—he or she is on God's side, and God does not like division. Doug, you have to show your people that they must not take sides over an individual or an issue. Once we take sides, it's human nature that we will try to justify our decision. We decide that our side is pure and good and the other side is evil and bad. What happens, though, is that both sides end up evil. They both develop attitudes that are not Christlike. A judgmental attitude is wrong no matter which side the person is on.

In any church division there are not just two groups—there are three. The third group is the host of people in the middle who keep quiet, refuse to take a side, and pray. The church can be healthy again when everyone moves over into the middle.

Doug, the pastor's responsibility is to help them move quietly back to the middle.

The challenge is to head off the division before it happens. I remember when we decided to replace the carpet in the sanctuary. The red carpet had been there for 30 years. Many of the frayed seams were held together with duct tape so folks wouldn't trip. We knew it was dangerous to walk in there—but we quickly realized it was even more dangerous to change the color.

A small decorating committee was appointed to select the new carpet. The time came for the work to be done. I knew that when the congregation assembled the next Sunday, the new carpet would be in place. I wasn't looking forward to that, so I made a speech the Sunday morning before the carpet was installed. It went something like this: "Next Sunday when you enter the sanctuary, the new carpet is going to be here. Some of you are going to love it, and some of you are going to hate it. But I tell you what I want us to do. No one is going to say 'I love this carpet.' No one is going to say 'I hate this carpet. Who in the world picked this out?' Everyone is going to say the same thing: 'Man—isn't this carpet safe!'"

Everyone laughed, and the next Sunday there were no complaints. All over the church, people were saying, "This sure is safe carpet!"

I don't remember hearing one negative comment, nor did I hear a positive one. Years later they still talk with fondness about their *safe* carpet.

I'm praying for you, Doug—praying that God will help you to be a "uniter" and not a "polarizer."

Pleased with the prospects,
BB

P. S. Hey, Doug—check out the wisdom of Solomon: "A brother offended is harder to be won than a strong city, And contentions are like the bars of a citadel" (Prov. 18:19, NASB). "Keeping away from strife is an honor for a man, But any fool will quarrel" (Prov. 20:3, NASB).

18

More and More Meetings

Dear Pastor Doug,

Have you noticed you seem to spend a lot of time in meetings? That's just part of the program. Meetings can be times of great blessing when the group comes together to dream for the future—or they can be painful.

I recall a monthly board meeting that was especially tense. The issue we debated is long gone from my memory, but I still remember the pressure I felt. As I recall, we were seated around folding tables positioned to form a rectangle with a large open space in the middle. I was getting nervous trying to figure out a way to cool the volatile situation. While twiddling my pen, it flew out of my hands into the open space at the center of the tables. The conversation stopped, and everyone looked at me to see how I planned to retrieve my pen. I pushed my chair back, got down on my knees, and crawled out to the pen. Then I crawled back to my seat.

It struck the board members funny to see their pastor in such an undignified situation. First came chuckles—then full-blown laughter. As I climbed into my chair, it dawned on me that the atmosphere in that room had completely changed in less than 30 seconds. The diversion stopped the wrangling, and we continued on with new freedom.

I learned a valuable lesson that day. When the meeting gets tight, be creative. Do or say something humorous to break the tension. Take a five-minute bathroom break, or have cake and cookies and coffee available for just such a time. Carol baked desserts for every board meeting I conducted during 20 years of pastoring. As a result, the members and the meetings were sweeter. Release the tension in those meetings any way you can, Doug.

Another annual meeting you'll face is that of the nominating committee for your church board. That meeting sometimes becomes difficult. Nominations for the board members begin with someone saying, "I nominate John for the board."

Someone else says, "Oh, no—I don't think that's a good idea. John has some bad habits that we don't agree with. He really wouldn't make a good board member."

Someone else says, "I nominate Sue."

Another board member responds, "Not a good idea. Sue is the biggest gossip in the church." It gets worse from there.

You can't allow your church members to be subjected to this kind of discussion and public embarrassment. The indictments may or may not be true, but that's not the point. These types of criticism shouldn't be voiced in an open meeting. It's not enough to say, "All that is said must stay in this room." You can't be sure that it will.

I suggest that when you begin the nominating committee meeting you set some guidelines. I always said, "Now, folks, I was wondering if you would give me a special privilege. You may nominate someone tonight that I know has a difficult situation or personal problem that would preclude him or her from serving on the board. Maybe you would give me the privilege of discreetly removing his or her name from the ballot. That way we will not have to embarrass anyone in this meeting." Nominating committees always gave me that privilege, and I rarely had to use it.

One time a fellow was nominated, and I knew he never gave a dime to the church. I did not speak up in the meeting and say, "That man doesn't tithe, and he has no right to serve on the board." But I went to the member in question and explained what had happened. It was an opportunity for us to have a great conversation about what's expected of church leaders. It was just between the two of us, and no one was injured in the process.

My prayer for you, Doug, is that God will give you wisdom as you conduct those meetings.

Pleased with the prospects,
BB

P. S. Hey, Doug—check out the wisdom of Solomon: "Without wood a fire goes out; without gossip a quarrel dies down" (Prov. 26:20). "A fool gives full vent to his anger, but a wise man keeps himself under control" (Prov. 29:11).

19

Insert Yourself

Dear Pastor Doug,

The other day I visited William, one of your fellow pastors, and he and I went out to lunch. While we made our trip to the salad-and-food bar, I noticed that he seemed to know everyone in the restaurant. This struck me as unusual for two reasons. One, William has only been pastoring in that city for a short time, and, two, he doesn't have an outgoing never-met-a-stranger-type personality. My curiosity was piqued enough that I said, "William, how do you know all these people?"

He responded, "Band Boosters."

"What?" I asked, perplexed.

"Band Boosters. My daughter plays an instrument in the band, and we parents support them."

William has learned a valuable lesson. Most people won't come to church just because the doors are open. A pastor must insert himself into his or her community. The more the pastor does that, the more contacts he or she will have, and the more people will find their way to his or her church. I'm sure William doesn't love carrying tubas and bass drums. He does it to help his daughter. And he meets people in his community.

Many pastors spend too much time in their offices with their books and computers. They need to be out and about with the people. Insert yourself into the community. Join some service organization, or get involved in neighborhood projects. If your kids are in sports, be there. Volunteer as chaplain for the hospital or police force. I always volunteered with the mortuaries in town if they needed a preacher or singer at late notice. There are a thousand ways to do it, and a thousand contacts and blessings will come to you in return.

Older ministers used to call this "personal work." Somehow it had been instilled in them that they needed to work with sinners, one-on-one, to win them to the Lord. I'll be forever thankful to Pastor Durrough, who many years ago took my brother, Roy, on as a project when he was away from the Lord. Every Saturday Pastor Durrough would go to my brother's house. He knew Roy wasn't always going to be receptive, but he went anyway. Roy was impressed by the faithfulness of this pastor in doing "personal work."

I have a pastor friend in Alabama who decided to win a man to the Lord. The man kept moving to get away from Pastor James. Undeterred, the pastor chased that man all over Winston County, praying and believing that he would find Christ. Years later, the man did find Christ and testified to the fact that it was because Pastor James never gave up on him.

Doug, it's so easy to spend your whole week with people who love you, but you must not. I challenge you to spend one day a week in "personal work." Bivocational pastors couldn't spend a whole day, but they could spend one evening. On this day or evening, be intentional about contacting sinners. Don't visit your church people. Plan to be with sinners during that day. You might spend a couple of hours praying and fasting for people who need the Lord and ask God to place in your mind who you should go see. He will! Ask Him to give you the opportunity to present the gospel to someone that day. He will! Call on young couples you have married and haven't seen in a long time. Call on the families of children you have dedicated. Have a cup of coffee with a stranger at McDonald's. Find a neighbor working in the yard and ask, "Do you know anybody who needs Jesus?" You never know what the answer to a question like that will be. Call someone that you haven't seen in a long time and say, "I was just thinking about you. How's everything going?" That may be just the opening they need to talk to you. There are many ways you can insert yourself into your community. You'll be greatly blessed.

Go get 'em, Doug! They probably won't just show up.

Pleased with the prospects,
BB

P. S. Hey, Doug—check out the wisdom of Solomon: "A little sleep, a little slumber, a little folding of the hands to rest—and poverty will come on

you like a bandit and scarcity like an armed man"
(Prov. 24:33-34).

20

Your Most Important Quality

Dear Pastor Doug,

Samuel Chadwick was a great preacher who believed in preparing his heart before entering the pulpit. Just before he entered the sanctuary, he would read the fifth chapter of Revelation. Try it next Sunday, Doug. "Worthy is the Lamb, who was slain, to receive power and wealth and wisdom and strength and honor and glory and praise! . . . To Him who sits on the throne and to the Lamb be praise and honor and glory and power, for ever and ever!" (Rev. 5:12-13). As you read that chapter, imagine yourself at the throne. You can't help but be lifted into heavenly places. Your spirit will then be ready to preach.

Not only is the quality of your spirit important as you enter the pulpit but also the quality of your spirit when you exit the pulpit. People will say positive things about your preaching, but don't let that affect you too much. Give the praise to God. People will also say negative things about you and find fault with your preaching. Don't let that affect you too much either. Give that to God also, and don't take it personally. If you've preached what God gave you, you don't need to be defensive or arrogant.

I had a conversation recently with a retired district superintendent. He told me about a difficult time in his life that occurred while he was pastoring. Another minister was making it difficult for him by saying things that were not true and was acting erratically. My friend made an appointment to meet with General Superintendent Hardy C. Powers and spent a couple of hours pouring out his heart to him about his problem colleague. Finally he was done talking and waited to receive the sage advice of the general superintendent. Dr. Powers simply said, "Friend, the quality of our spirit is our stock-in-trade in the ministry." My friend waited for Dr. Powers to elaborate, but that was it. That's all Dr. Powers said. At first, my friend was disappointed with the answer, but after pondering it later that day, he realized the profound importance of it.

Doug, it's all we have. If you lose the good spirit God has blessed you with, you're finished. As you think back on the great ministers you've known, you'll realize that they all had different gifts and different preaching styles, but they all had the same beautiful Christlike spirit. That spirit burned brightly in the good times and the bad.

You may also remember some bitter preachers. Maybe it was because they had been hurt so many times they just couldn't shake the bitterness. Sadly, that kind of spirit will not win people to Jesus. It will repulse them.

Some preachers have trouble understanding authority. They seem to believe that the mere title of "Pastor" brings with it respect and authority. But authority does not automatically come with the title. It comes with a certain temperament. One cannot expect or ask for authority.

Real authority can't be demanded. It must be given. It will be given to the preacher who earns it by loving people, by serving people, by depending on other people, and by trusting people. That's the kind of spirit Jesus exhibited. He was a man with great authority.

No matter the pain or the glory, Doug, keep a good spirit. "The quality of our spirit is our stock-in-trade in the ministry."

Pleased with the prospects,
BB

P. S. Hey, Doug—check out the wisdom of Solomon: "It is not good to eat too much honey, nor is it honorable to seek one's own honor" (Prov. 25:27).

21

A Defining Moment

Dear Pastor Doug,

Have you noticed in recent years that one particular two-word phrase has become overused and overworked? *Defining moment.* In their quest to make news momentous, journalists have begun to see a myriad of moments as *defining moments.* Politicians, talk-show hosts, and even ordinary people want instant history. So we call even mundane moments *defining moments.*

Recent years have been filled with defining moments: The Oklahoma City bombing, the new millennium, September 11, Operation Iraqi Freedom. I don't know how many times America can get defined, but I'm sure we'll use that phrase over and over gain.

At the risk of overworking the phrase even more, I must tell you that I've had a few defining moments as well. Let me tell you about one such moment. As a young pastor, I was quick to want to set everyone straight. I remember a Wednesday night Bible study class when a new fellow named Al showed up. He was a brand-new father. In the lesson, we talked about how children are born in sin and possess a sin nature. He just couldn't fathom that his beautiful little daughter was sinful. So almost in defense of his flesh and blood, he entered the discussion: "Babies aren't born in sin," he proclaimed. "My little girl is pure and holy."

Somehow I thought my orthodoxy was on the line in front of the more theologically astute in the room. So I tried to kindly explain to him the error of his thinking, that the Bible clearly teaches that children carry within them a carnal, sinful nature. Well, I guess I set him straight—he never came back.

I wish I had that night to do over. My approach would be different. I would talk about prevenient grace. I would have said something like this: "I know what you mean. That little one of yours is holy and pure in a very real sense. She hasn't reached the age of accountability yet. She's wearing the protection and righteousness of Jesus Christ. If she were to die, she would go straight to heaven." I would have protected him more. He may have come back.

In my youth I spoke a lot about judgment. The older I get, the more I want to talk about grace. I want my defining moments to be filled with grace. Oh, it's true that we need to know the reality of judgment. But, Doug, be quick to throw some grace in there. You'll get farther with grace.

Pleased with the prospects,
BB

P. S. Hey Doug—check out the wisdom of Solomon: "Who can say, 'I have kept my heart pure; I am clean and without sin'?" (Prov. 20:9).

22

Healing and Holiness

Dear Pastor Doug,

Do you remember the first healing service we had in Tampa? We invited people to come forward for healing, and we prayed for each one. It took us two hours to finish, but the people stayed in rapt attention. God didn't heal all of them in an instant, but we did what He told us to do. We simply asked Him to bring healing.

He did heal some. Remember Michael? He came for prayer. He was battling paranoid thoughts and hearing strange voices. Doug, I checked with him the other day. He told me that he hadn't heard any of those voices since that healing service. It's been seven years! Praise God! He still heals people, and we must give Him opportunity to work.

Unfortunately, we preachers have allowed the faith healers on television to steal something beautiful from us. Because we don't want to be identified with some that are charlatans, we may have unconsciously backed away from offering divine healing to our people. But we still believe that God heals, and He wants us to ask for His healing.

Have you had a healing service lately, Doug? If not, I urge you to schedule one. Tell your people that you're going to have a healing service, and encourage them to be praying. When you gather at the appointed time, preach a message on healing. It won't be difficult to find a text—Jesus was involved in healings often.

You may want to preach about the three times that Jesus healed blind men. He dealt with each of them differently. The passage gives us insight about how Jesus is healing people today. The first instance is Matt. 9:27-30. In that passage, Jesus healed two blind men instantaneously. Today some healings occur right before our eyes as well.

The second passage is Mark 8:22-26. There you will discover a blind man receiving help. The Lord spit in his eyes and asked him if he could see. He said he saw men as trees walking. In other words, after Jesus touched him, his vision was better but still blurred. The Lord had to touch him a second time. That intimates the Lord sometimes brings healing in a gradual way.

The third experience is in the ninth chapter of John. Jesus told the man to walk through the city with a layer of moistened clay on his eyes to the pool of Siloam. You might consider that clay as medicine was applied by Christ. The Lord asked him to humble himself and walk through the city with mud on his face. It was an unusual command, but the man obeyed.

There's no set pattern to bring healing, no set words or magic phrases that we must say. In all three cases the illness was the same, but the cure was different. The sovereignty of God can't be overruled. We just simply come to Him and ask for healing. Sometimes the Lord chooses to heal us. Sometimes He knows that His kingdom is better served by our living graciously with a "thorn in the flesh," as the apostle Paul did.

After you've preached your message on healing, simply invite the people to come forward, anoint them, and pray for them. It will be a thrill to see God work.

We must not only offer our people healing—we must offer them spiritual wholeness. We are Holiness preachers, Doug. We believe that Jesus not only saves our souls and heals our bodies, but He also sanctifies us through and through. We can be Spirit-filled Christians. This isn't just a topic that we mention once a year on Pentecost Sunday—it is our theme! I urge you to hold up the holy life before your people constantly. Someone has said that the only way to keep a broken vessel full is to keep it under the tap. The only way for our congregations to experience a Spirit-filled life is to often remind them of the possibility and the potential of holiness. They must keep their lives under the tap of the flow of the Spirit so that their vessels can remain full.

Don't be reticent about sharing your own story. Let them hear how God dealt with you. Give opportunity for those in the congregation who have a clear testimony of entire sanctification to share their stories in church services. It will make the experience of heart holiness seem more attainable for all who hear.

My prayer is that every Holiness preacher will ask God to renew his or her passion for preaching what John Wesley called the life of "perfect love."

Doug, while you're offering them healing for their bodies, offer them healing for their souls. "He who calls you is faithful, who also will do it" (1 Thess. 5:24, NKJV).

Pleased with the prospects,
BB

P. S. Hey, Doug—check out the wisdom of Solomon: "He who pursues righteousness and love finds life, prosperity and honor" (Prov. 21:21).

23

Family Matters

Dear Pastor Doug,

Let me tell you what I miss most about our home in Tampa. We lived there six years, and it was a beautiful home. But I don't miss the swimming pool. I surely enjoyed the great room and fireplace, but I can get along without them. I certainly don't miss cutting the grass on that large corner lot.

What I miss is the wall in the laundry room. I passed that wall every day and looked at it often. There were a bunch of pencil marks on that wall that I can never duplicate and will never see again. Not ever. Not in any house.

My son and daughter each grew a couple of feet while we were living there. And every month or so we got out the pencil and backed them up against the wall and said, "Straighten up. . . . Put your head back—back farther. . . . Hey—take those shoes off." And we marked their progress.

Lincoln was especially proud of the mark proving he had outgrown his big sister, Keely. Then there was a mark when he passed his mom and finally his dad. I just kind of tolerated it.

Man, I miss that wall! I miss the memories of those measurement marks. I was thinking about you and how sometimes growing is painful and the passage of time hurts. But God is teaching you something in each of these growth spurts. Mark them and thank God for them! Someday they'll be your best memories.

When Carol and I arrived at our first church, we were excited to apply everything I had learned at seminary. It didn't take long to realize that some of what I learned about operating a church didn't fit. A small church doesn't operate like a business, and the pastor is not a CEO.

The smaller church operates more like a family. The people there don't want the pastor to organize them or inspect them. They just want to be loved. They just want the pastor to "mark the wall" and enjoy growing and living with the church family.

That being the case, as a pastor you'll need to step out of the office and get out among the family. Of course, you'll need to preach well. But you'll need to spend much of your time just building relationships. You'll want to bring about changes in the church, of course. But that won't be accomplished as much in board meetings as it will in relationships. When the people feel you're part of the family, they'll be more open to your ideas.

If you have a good idea, bring it up at the next board meeting. I warn you that they probably will not make a decision to adopt it right then. Church board members in smaller churches want to think about new ideas. They want to talk about it with their family members. You may want to bring up a new idea over coffee with a few of the board members. If it's a good idea, someone will bring it up at a future board meeting after there's been time for the idea to filter through the congregation. Good ideas will surface again. That's the way the small church operates.

You're accepted into the family as you get involved in personal lives. I've done a lot of things that I wasn't taught in seminary in order to build relationships. I spent one day holding little piglets up by the hind legs as one of my parishioners castrated them. I don't recommend this—my hands had a musty pig smell for weeks. But it was worth it, because that farmer and I were brothers from then on. I delivered calves, fed cattle, walked two miles underground into an ore mine, scooped rocks, hunted deer and elk, climbed a mountain, helped folks move furniture, carried boiler pipe, went camping (Carol was not excited about that one), helped the coroner pick up dead bodies (*I* was not excited about that one), and visited innumerable offices, factories, schools, and workplaces —all in the name of building relationships.

Doug, these are some of my best memories in ministry. I was intentionally trying to be part of the family. They graciously took me in and thereby became part of my family. It doesn't happen quickly. It takes a while for trust to build. Just be patient.

Soon, when they have problems, you'll be the first one they think to call. You'll be thrilled to get up from your desk, leave the office, and go to where they are. You're about to make a new mark on the laundry room wall. They're family, you know!

Pleased with the prospects,
BB

P. S. Hey, Doug—check out the wisdom of Solomon: "The generous man will be prosperous, And he who waters will himself be watered" (Prov. 11:25, NASB).

24

Painful People Can Be a Pain

Dear Pastor Doug,

A lady named Evelyn attended one of the churches I pastored. She has since gone to be with the Lord. I remember how shocked I was the first time I talked with her—her life was painful and difficult. She struggled both emotionally and mentally. Every few months she needed to talk with me, and the story was always the same. I could tell she was in great pain, because the tears flowed as she talked. She was convinced that all the stories she watched on television were her own. She had written them. She had lived them. Over and over she said to me, "Pastor Bob, they're stealing my stories. I'm the one who should be on television. I should be getting credit for those stories."

I learned not to try to correct her. I do wish I could have changed her, but it was far beyond my ability. I did what I could: I just listened and listened and listened. Then we prayed together, and she was all right for a while.

At first I chafed whenever Evelyn called needing to talk. But eventually I realized that this was my opportunity to give a gift to a hurting lady who didn't have much of anything in this world.

One thing I have noticed about you, Doug, is that God has given you a lot of patience when dealing with people. What a great gift that is! You'll meet some very difficult people in your ministry. They won't mean to be difficult, but they will be.

Some folks just have to share their opinions—about everything. It's painful to listen. But you can. Listen respectfully, thank them for their input, and then go do what you feel is best. You don't have to do what they say. Many folks just want to be heard. God can give you grace to just simply listen.

Sometimes people will say hurtful things to you. Some will be cruel and mean. But many times not even they believe what they're saying. They just want your ear. Give them your ear—but don't allow it to break your heart.

Here's a little mental exercise that Carol and I have employed through the years, and it works for us. Remember conversations you've had with a mentally ill person? You basically discounted what he or she said. The person maybe said some mean things to you, but you didn't take them personally because you just kept reminding yourself, *Well, he's [she's] not thinking straight. He [She] doesn't know what he [she] is saying. I don't have to take these things personally, because he [she] isn't capable of making a sound judgment.*" You can manage painful words if you don't allow them to penetrate.

Many times after a painful encounter, Carol

and I have looked at each other, smiled, and in unison said, "He [She] must have a brain tumor." That's all that needs to be said between us. We don't say it derogatorily or with a mean spirit. It is just our way of releasing the pain. Then we can march on unaffected.

Perhaps you're thinking, *That sure is cold!* But I believe it's the caring way to work. So many people need our care. Even those who are difficult to deal with need us. We can't just ignore them. We must learn to cope so that a few painful people don't steal our joy and our enthusiasm for ministry. We can't change them. We just love them as they are until God decides to transform them or take them home.

Pleased with the prospects,
BB

P. S. Hey, Doug—check out the wisdom of Solomon: "A constant dripping on a day of steady rain And a contentious woman are alike; He who would restrain her restrains the wind, And grasps oil with his right hand" (Prov. 27:15-16, NASB).

25

Three Strands

Dear Pastor Doug and Joni,

This is to both of you. Doug, next to the Lord, Joni will be your best comforter, critic, cohort, and colleague. In the providence of God, you selected very well, and she had the wisdom to say *yes* to your proposal.

Daily I thank God for Carol. I first looked into the depths of her green eyes 30 years ago, and I'm still not over the spell of it. We couldn't do what we do without these faithful mates. If they suddenly decided to break up the teamwork, we would be hard-pressed to continue.

So, Doug, cherish her. Treat her tenderly. Protect her. Shield her from some of the pain. You don't need to tell her all the hurtful things you know in the congregation. Take time for her. With every word, make her feel that you believe that you're the most fortunate man alive to have her.

Joni, be his biggest booster. After every service, Carol came to me and said, "Wow, what a great sermon! I don't know how you do it. It was even better than last Sunday." I knew it wasn't true, but I sure appreciated her saying so. If you have some constructive criticism, wait until Tuesday to tell him. He'll be able to handle it better then.

Keep every confidence shared with you. Don't tell what you know. Many pastors have been destroyed by wives who could not keep secrets. In the same way, many pastors have destroyed their own ministry by not keeping the confidences shared with them.

Always try to keep Sunday peaceful around the parsonage. I know it's tough with little children, but it will preserve his emotional energy for preaching. Be his biggest prayer warrior. As you pray, God will release His power in greater measure on his ministry.

Treat each other kindly, with great respect and honor. They're watching you out there. You're modeling a Christlike marriage and home all the time.

Forty years from now, when you come down to the end of your ministry, some of the greatest pleasures that the two of you will enjoy will be the memories of ministry. I heard Nancy Reagan being interviewed on television recently. She was talking about her husband, former United States president Ronald Reagan, who now has Alzheimer's disease. She said that the hardest part of her life now was that she could not share her memories with her husband. His memories are gone. She talked about the fact that when you come down to the end of life, your shared memories are wonderful blessings.

My mom and dad have been married for more than 60 years, and they have made many memories through those years. One Sunday morning they were visiting Carol and me. The four of us were driving to church when my dad surprised us. Since he's an unusually quiet person, when he does open his mouth, all conversation stops to hear what he has to say. He had a memory to share that morning—a 76-year-old one. "I was 14," Dad said, "and that April morning I rode my bike to school just like always. It doesn't usually snow in Nebraska in April, so I could hardly believe it. There was so much snow that I couldn't ride my bike home that afternoon. I put the bike on my back and walked home on the railroad track." And he paused. I remember thinking, *What a strange thing to say!* and I wondered why he was telling this story. Then he added, "That's the day your mom was born."

Now, I knew that Mom had been born 50 miles away—in Kansas—and the two families didn't even know each other. So I said, "What? How could you have known that was the day Mom was born?"

"Because when she was born, her mother looked over at the bedroom window and saw that the snow was piling up above the windowsill. It was one of the worst April snowstorms ever in Kansas and Nebraska. So, you see, I remember the day your mother was born. That was a big day in my life."

The tenderness of that moment struck me. My dad, often reclusive in his thoughts, doesn't express his feelings much. In a cryptic sort of way he was sending a message to my mother in the backseat. "I love you, Margaret. The day you were born is a precious memory for me."

Doug and Joni, you're a great team. Any church will be pleased to have you in their parsonage. The Lord has good things planned for you! While you're traveling through the adventure of ministry, take the time to make some memories. You'll enjoy them as long as you live.

Pleased with the prospects,
BB

P. S. Hey, Doug and Joni—check out the wisdom of Solomon: "Though one may be overpowered, two can defend themselves. A cord of three strands is not quickly broken" (Eccles. 4:12).

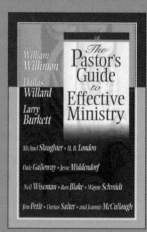